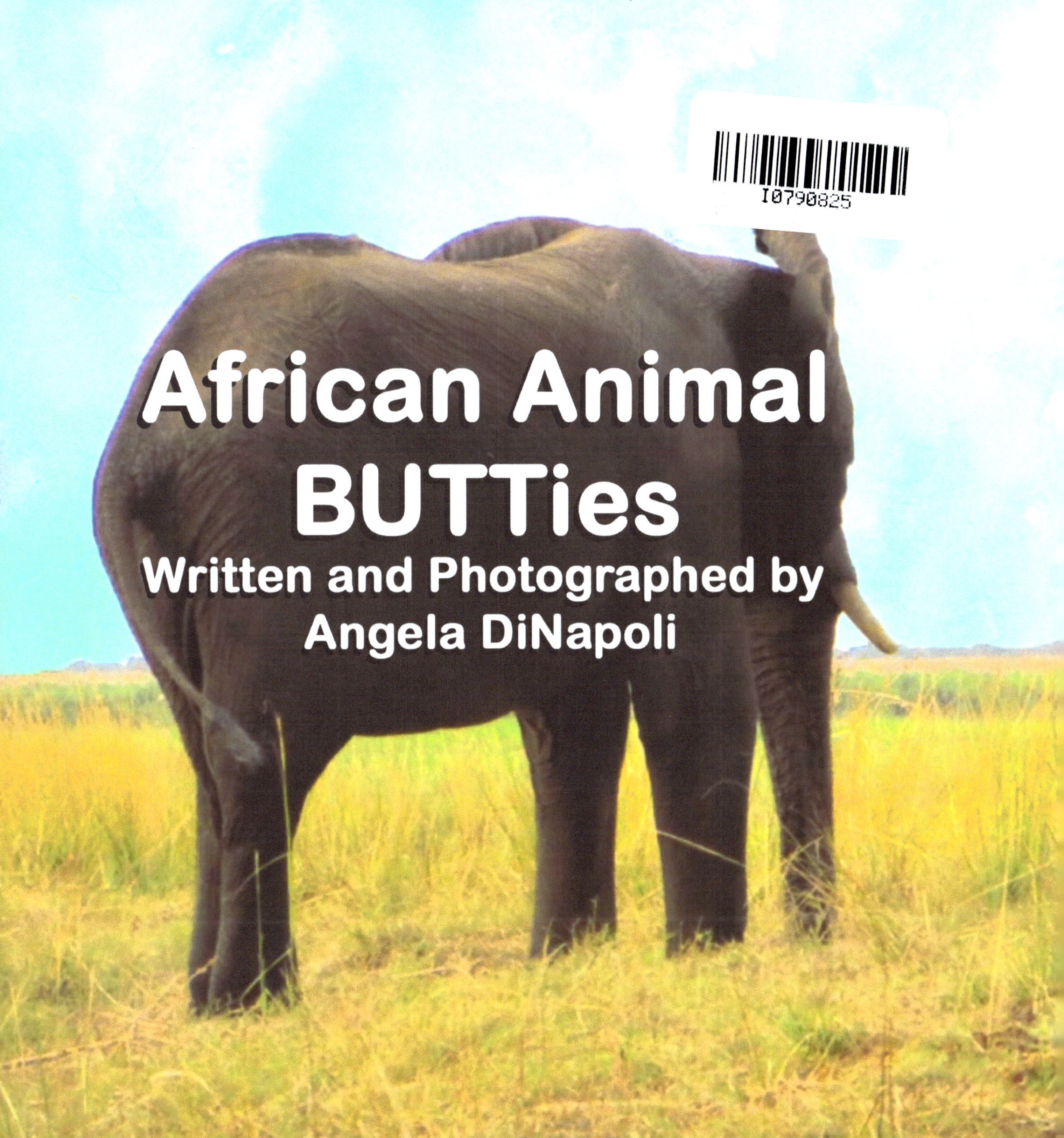
African Animal
BUTTies
Written and Photographed by
Angela DiNapoli
I0790825

NOTE FROM THE AUTHOR/PHOTOGRAPHER

ACKNOWLEDGMENT

I thank my son, Jon DiNapoli (artofdino.com), for his creative editing, colorful backgrounds, and overall suppo
and suggestions. Without his assistance, this book would not exist.
His artistic talent cannot be underestimated.

DEDICATION

This book is dedicated to my "buttie", Marilyn, for making my trip to Africa possible and fun

Animals never stop for poses.
Taking pictures is a trick.
From their heads to their toes,
This photographer was not so quick.

I focused on the faces
So my shots would be clear cut.
As often was the case,
I mostly got their butts.

It's hard to take a shot
When animals are in motion.
They roam around a lot
That's why my crazy notion.

Hope you enjoy this butt book.
I tried my best, you'll see.
Of all the pics I took,
These butts were best for me!

Penguin's butt likes to slide.

While lion's butt has much pride.

Stork's butt touches the sky.

Water buck's looks like a bull's eye.

Rhino's butt is kind of rough.

Dassie's butt is
covered in fluff.

Elephants' butts will top the scale.

**Mongoose's butt
leaves a trail.**

Giraffe's butt is high off the ground.

Sunbird's butt is upside down.

Guinea fowl's butt
has polka dots.

Cheetah's butt
has lots of spots.

Sable antelopes' butts are mostly white.

African Darter's butt takes to flight.

Warthogs' butts are rather stumpy.

Nile croc's butt is
very bumpy.

Hippo's butt is fat and broad.

Impala's M lettered
butt is odd.

Zebra's butt is white and black.

Baboon's butt
shows a crack.

Kudu's butt is tight and neat.

Wildebeest's butt is
not so sweet.

Kingfisher's butt has a bluish hue.

Cape Buffalo's butt is
hard to view.

But the best butts
that I met...

Were on the people
I won't forget!

Guess the Butts

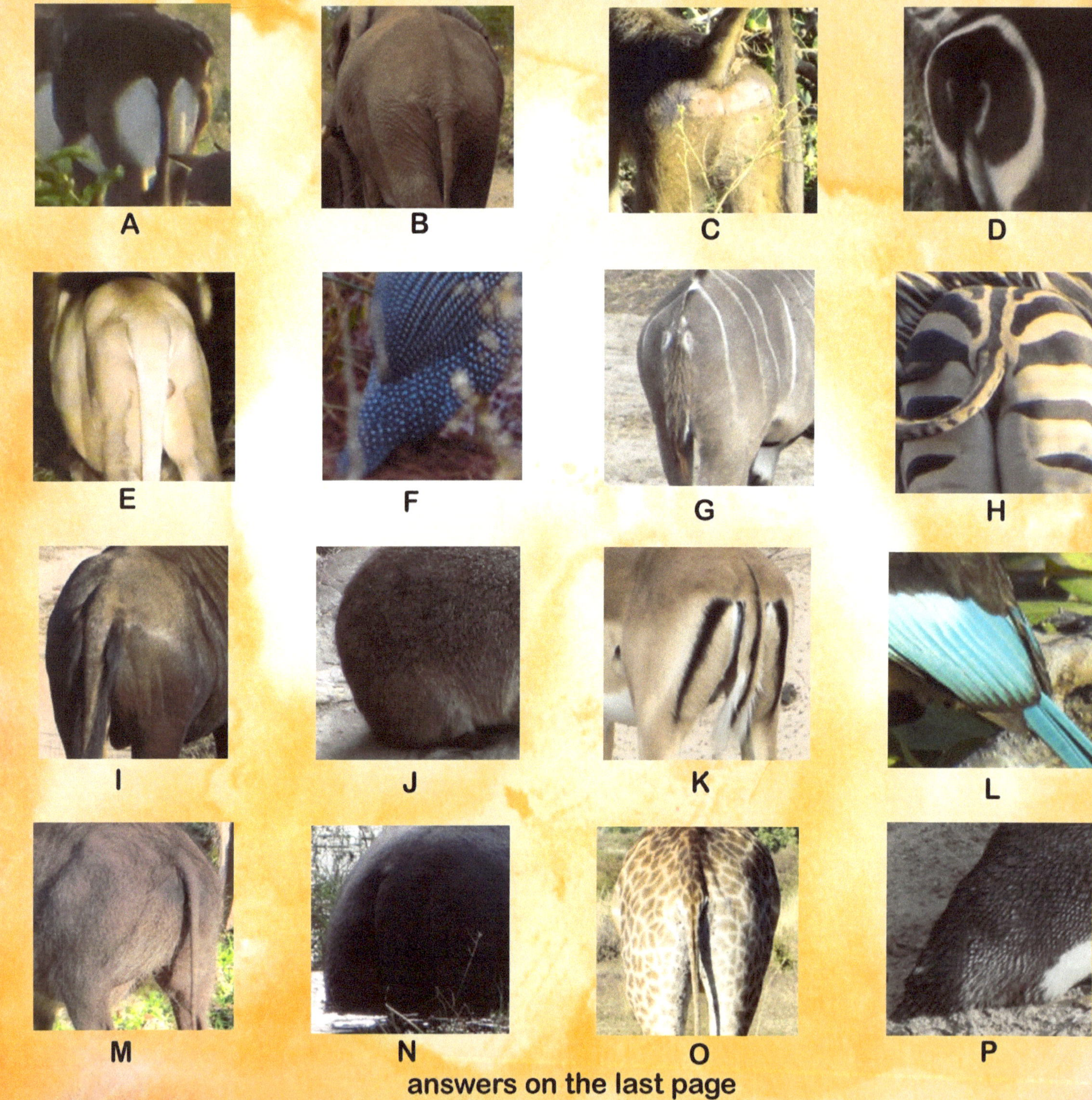

A B C D E F G H I J K L M N O P

answers on the last page

NOTHING "BUTT" THE FACTS!
AFRICAN ANIMALS
(NOTE: All life spans stated are in the wild not in captivity.)

AFRICAN DARTER BIRD (SNAKEBIRD)

This bird has a thin, long neck that can turn and twist in unusual ways. It swims with only its neck above water, which looks like a snake. It has a pointed beak to stab fish. Its feathers are not waterproof so it often sits on land with its wings spread out to dry.

BABOON

This monkey is an omnivore with a long dog-like muzzle, strong jaw, and sharp teeth. It lives in groups or troops of 20 or more members. It can make 30 different sounds like grunts, screams, and barks. The life span in the wild is 30 years.

CAPE BUFFALO

This bovine (cattle) animal has fused horns shaped like a question mark. Cape buffalo travel in herds of a few thousand animals and are very protective and dangerous. They are herbivores and like to lick termite mounds. Their life span is about 20 years.

CARNIVORE

Animal that eats only meats such as insects and all other animals.

CHEETAH

This cat is the fastest animal on land running up to 70 miles per hour, which it can reach in 3 seconds. Although it catches its prey quickly, it takes up to 25 minutes to kill the prey due to its small jaw and teeth. This carnivore hunts during the day. Cheetahs cannot roar, but instead make a chirping sound. Their life span is 7 to 12 years.

DASSIE

These herbivorous mammals are also called hyraxes. They have soft fur and short tails. Though they look like a rodent, dassies are distant relatives of elephants. They have rubbery pads on their feet, which help them move around steep, rocky surfaces. Dassies can whistle, mew, and shriek. Their life span is about 7 years.

ELEPHANT

This is the largest land animal. Elephants are herbivores that can eat over 300 pounds of food a day and poop 200 pounds of manure a day. The female has a pregnancy of 22 months, and an elephant calf at birth can weigh 230 pounds. The elephant's trunk has 40,000 muscles to help smell, grab things, drink, dig, and balance itself. Elephants have a life span of about 70 years.

GIRAFFE

Giraffes are the tallest animals in the world. A baby giraffe at birth is about 6 feet tall. Adult giraffes can reach a height of 20 feet. They are herbivores that especially like to eat Acacia leaves. The giraffe's tongue can be 20 inches long. A giraffe's life span is about 25 years.

GUINEA FOWL

This bird is a ground dwelling omnivore, which feeds on worms, insects, reptiles, spiders, berries, seeds, and roots. The guinea fowl is a very social animal and roosts in flocks. This bird is a strong flyer but prefers to run around. The guinea fowl has a life span of 10 to 20 years.

HERBIVORE

Animal that eats only plants such as leaves, grass, flowers, seeds, roots, fruits, bark, pollen, and more.

HIPPO

The hippopotamus is called the "river horse". It spends most of the day under water where it can hold its breath for over 5 minutes. The hippo is an herbivore eating about 150 pounds of grass a day. Its skin produces its own natural sunscreen. The hippo life span is 40 to 50 years.

IMPALA

The impala is the most common and most graceful of the antelopes. Impalas can run fast and leap 10 feet in the air traveling a distance of 33 feet.   They are herbivores living in herds of all females or all males. Their life span is 12 to 15 years.

KINGFISHER (WOODLAND)

The woodland kingfisher is a carnivore feeding mostly on insects but will eat lizards, millipedes, frogs, snakes, and some small birds. This bird usually nests in tree cavities left by woodpeckers especially in Acacia trees. They are often alone but can be sometimes found in small groups.

KUDU

The kudu is a type of antelope with long spiral horns that twist 2.5 times. Kudus have white stripes and spots on their bodies. They are herbivores and can survive a long time without water. The kudu is the loudest of the antelopes making a barking sound. The life span is about 8 years.

LION

Lions are the biggest, most social cats living in groups called prides. Male lions come and go, but the lioness keeps the pride together. She hunts and takes care of the cubs. A lion roar can be heard 5 miles away. Lions sleep up to 18 hours a day and mostly hunt at night. The life span is 12 years.

MONGOOSE

The mongoose is a small mammal with a striped coat and ringed tail. The mongoose is a carnivore eating insects, worms, lizards, birds, and snakes. They are immune to snake poisons. They live in abandoned burrows. When they are in danger, they make a high pitched giggling noise. The life span is 4 years.

NILE CROCODILE

The Nile crocodile is the largest reptile in Africa. It can be as long as 16 feet but moves at lightning speeds. It can hold its breath under water for 10 minutes and go months without food. The skin is armor-like for protection. The life span is 45 years.

OMNIVORE

Animal that eats both plants and animals.

PENGUIN

The African penguin is also known as the "jackass" penguin because of the braying sound it makes. These carnivores can dive up to 400 feet and hold their breath for 2.5 minutes. They feed on fish, squid, and shellfish. They are endangered due to overfishing, pollution, and loss of habitat. They live in colonies and mate for life. The life span is 10 to 20 years.

RHINOCEROS

The name Rhinoceros means "nose horn". Its horn is made out of keratin like hair and fingernails. Rhinos have thick protective skins and have no natural predators except for humans who poach them for their horns. The white rhino is nearly endangered. They are herbivores that travel in a group called a "crash". They communicate with each other by smelling piles of dung. The life span is 40 years.

SABLE ANTELOPE

These endangered antelopes are herbivores feeding mostly on tree leaves. They have ridged, curved horns that are about 5 feet long, which they use to defend themselves against predators. They live in herds of 10 to 30 members. The life span is up to 18 years.

STORK (MARABOU)

This stork has almost a 10-foot wingspan, which is the largest in the world. It is a carnivore feeding on dead animals, rotting materials, and even poop. It has a baldhead, so blood from its prey does not get caught on his head while eating. It ha hollow leg and toe bones for easier flying. The life span is 25 years.

SUNBIRD

The sunbird is an omnivore that feeds on nectar and fruit but also insects and spiders. It has a long curved bill and tubular tongue to reach the nectar. It helps in pollination. Its flight is fast due to short wings and a long tail. This bird stays in the same habitat al year living in pairs or small family groups. The life span is 7 years.

WARTHOG

The warthog is a relative of the pig, and gets its name for the fleshy bumps on its face. It has two pairs of huge tusks, which are used for digging and fighting. It is a herbivore, eating mostly grass. It has poor eyesight but excellent senses for smelling and hearing. It makes grunting, squealing sounds. The life span is 15 years.

WATERBUCK

The waterbuck is a large antelope. Only the males have horns about 40 inches long. The white bulls-eye on the butt helps the herd keep together when fleeing an enemy. They have an oily coat that smells bad which helps then find a mate, makes their coat waterproof, and keeps away predators. The waterbuck is a herbivore that grazes near water which it drinks several times a day. The life span is about 15 years.

WILDEBEEST

The wildebeests are also called gnus and are one of the largest antelopes though they look more like cattle. The wildebeests are herbivores and travel in large herds to find food and water. Migratory groups can have over a million wildebeests. After a few minutes of being born, a baby wildebeest or calf can run. After a few days, the calf can keep up with the pace of the herd. The life span is 20 years.

ZEBRA

The zebra is part of the same family as the horse and donkey. When being chased by a predator, the zebra runs from side to side for speeds up to 40 miles per hour. Each zebra has its own unique stripe pattern, kind of like an individual's fingerprint. Zebras sleep standing up and in a close group. The life span is 25 years.

Answers for Guess The Butts!

A. Sable Antelope	B. Elephant	C. Baboon	D. Waterbuck
E. Lion	F. Guinea Fowl	G. Kudu	H. Zebra
I. Wildebeest	J. Dassie	K. Impala	L. Kingfisher
M. Warthog	N. Hippo	O. Giraffe	P. Penguin